FEB - 9 2017

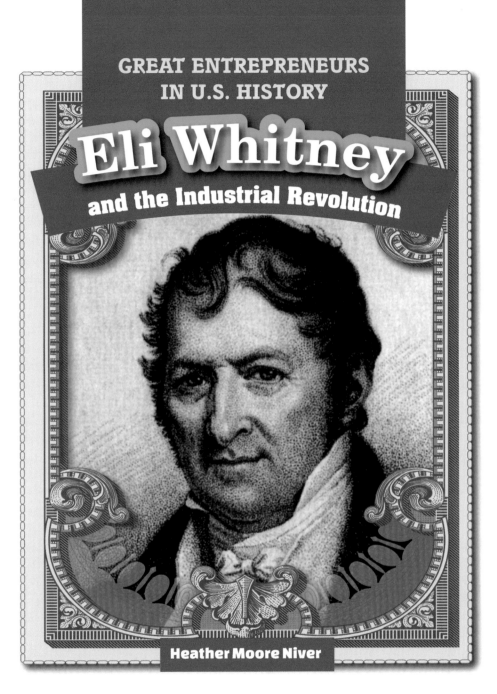

GREAT ENTREPRENEURS
IN U.S. HISTORY

Eli Whitney
and the Industrial Revolution

Heather Moore Niver

PowerKiDS
press™

New York

Published in 2017 by The Rosen Publishing Group, Inc.
29 East 21st Street, New York, NY 10010

First Edition

Editor: Sarah Machajewski
Book Design: Mickey Harmon

Photo Credits: Cover, pp. 1–4, 6–10, 12–22, 24, 26–28, 30–32 (series design) Melodist/Shutterstock.com; cover (Whitney), pp. 1, 11 Everett Historical/Shutterstock.com, p. 5 Stock Montage/Contributor/Archive Photos/Getty Images; p. 7 American School/Getty Images; p. 8 f11photo/Shutterstock.com; pp. 9, 20 MPI/Stringer/Getty Images; pp. 13, 15 Fritz Goro/Contributor/The LIFE Picture Collection/Getty Images; p. 17 https://en.wikipedia.org/wiki/Eli_Whitney#/media/File:Whitney_Gin.jpg; p. 19 (top) © North Wind Picture Archives/Alamy.com; p. 19 (bottom revolver) courtesy of the Tennessee State Library & Archives; p. 21 https://commons.wikimedia.org/wiki/File:Eli_Whitney_milling_machine_1818-001.png; p. 23 bikeriderlondon/Shutterstock.com; p. 25 https://en.wikipedia.org/wiki/Eli_Whitney#/media/File:Eli_Whitney_Gun_Factory_William_Giles_Munson_1827.jpg; p. 27 https://en.wikipedia.org/wiki/Eli_Whitney#/media/File:EliWhitneyGraveSouthSideGroveStCemeteryNewHavenCT04152008.JPG; p. 29 https://commons.wikimedia.org/wiki/File:Eli_Whitney_by_Samuel_Finley_Breese_Morse_1822.jpeg.

Library of Congress Cataloging-in-Publication Data

Names: Niver, Heather Moore, author.
Title: Eli Whitney and the Industrial Revolution / Heather Moore Niver.
Description: New York : PowerKids Press, [2017] | Series: Great entrepreneurs in U.S. history | Includes index.
Identifiers: LCCN 2016016331 | ISBN 9781499421231 (paperback) | ISBN 9781499421255 (library bound) | ISBN 9781499421248 (6 pack)
Subjects: LCSH: Whitney, Eli, 1765-1825–Juvenile literature. | Cotton gins and ginning–United States–History–Juvenile literature. | Inventors–United States–Biography–Juvenile literature. | Industrial revolution–United States–History–Juvenile literature.
Classification: LCC TS1570.W4 N58 2017 | DDC 609.2 [B] –dc23
LC record available at https://lccn.loc.gov/2016016331

Manufactured in the United States of America

CPSIA Compliance Information: Batch #BS16PK: For Further Information contact Rosen Publishing, New York, New York at 1-800-237-9932

Contents

Man of Many Talents

Eli Whitney wore many hats in his life: inventor, mechanical engineer, and manufacturer. He is best remembered as the inventor of the cotton gin, which was a revolutionary machine that offered a faster way to separate cotton fibers from the seeds.

The cotton gin transformed the American economy, but it wasn't Whitney's only contribution to history. In fact, his method of producing **muskets** made him his fortune. Because of this system, muskets no longer had to be made one at a time, and individual parts could be used in different muskets—not just in one. Whitney's willingness to think creatively and his refusal to give up when he didn't succeed changed the way American goods would be produced forever.

What Was the Industrial Revolution?

The Industrial Revolution was a period of history when the economy changed from being based on farming and agriculture to being based on **industry** and manufacturing. The Industrial Revolution began in Great Britain in the 1700s and soon spread around the world. This revolution changed the way things had been done for centuries. Many important inventions came out of the Industrial Revolution, including a tool called the spinning jenny, better steam engines, and the cotton gin.

5

Eli's Early Life

Eli Whitney was born on December 8, 1765, and grew up on a farm near Westboro, Massachusetts. His father was a farmer and a local judge. His mother was often sick. She died when Whitney was about 11 years old.

As a child, Whitney was known for being curious and asking a lot of questions. He always asked for more information. He liked watching his father work in his shop, where he built tools and objects for the farm and house. It wasn't long before Whitney started building things himself.

Whitney grew up during the American Revolution. Great Britain refused to import nails into the colony during the war, so Whitney began making them in his father's shop. By the age of 14, he had a very successful business.

The American Revolution

The American Revolution began in 1775 and lasted until 1783. American colonists were unhappy with the way Great Britain treated them. They felt they were denied their rights as British citizens and were angry over the taxes Great Britain passed on many goods, including sugar, tea, and paper. After years of unfair treatment, colonists decided they wanted their independence. They fought for the right to become their own country—the United States of America.

Massachusetts was a center of activity during the American Revolution. Westboro was close to Lexington and Concord, where the first shots of the war were fired.

School and Work

Whitney's work as a boy taught him important lessons about business and how marketplaces work. He had a **knack** for knowing what people needed and how to give it to them. In addition to nails, he also successfully made canes and hatpins—everyday items that people needed.

In May 1789, Whitney entered Yale College. Today, it's called Yale University. At Yale, he studied

Yale University today

Whitney learned a lot about doing experiments during his years at Yale College, pictured here in the 1700s.

science and technology, which was then called "the applied arts." He graduated in the fall of 1792. Whitney moved to the South to accept a job as a teacher, but the job fell through. He was left without money, a job, or a home. However, in the South, he would learn about some serious problems farmers faced—problems he could fix.

Friends and Cotton

Fortunately for Whitney, he met a woman named Catherine Greene while he was in Georgia. She owned a plantation. A plantation is a large farm on which crops such as cotton, tobacco, and sugarcane are grown. The Greene plantation was managed by a man named Phineas Miller, who was from Connecticut and had also studied at Yale. Miller and Whitney soon became friends.

While he was at the plantation, Whitney observed the world around him. He noticed that cotton producers in the South had some problems. Newly built **textile** factories created a big demand for cotton, but southern farmers weren't selling enough to meet the need. There weren't any cheap or quick methods of processing cotton, and farmers had a hard time making a **profit**.

Whitney's business sense allowed him to observe that both farmers and factory owners needed a way to get cotton cheaply and quickly. His solution would go on to change life in the South for years to come.

Sticky Problems

When Whitney arrived in Georgia, farmers were growing two types of cotton. With both kinds, the plant's cotton fiber had to be separated from its seeds. Long-staple cotton was easy to work with, but it could only be grown along the coast. Short-staple cotton grew well inland, but it had very sticky green seeds that took a long time to remove from the soft cotton **bolls**. Enslaved people were forced to do this time-consuming work.

Whitney was determined to figure out how to help the short-staple cotton producers. Catherine Greene supported his idea and helped him pay for it, too. But Whitney also knew that if he could help these farmers, he could make a bit of money for himself.

When Whitney saw the need for a quicker way to process cotton, he began working out a way to solve the problem. This is Whitney's workshop where he developed ideas such as the cotton gin.

The Rise of Slavery

While the cotton gin made a once-suffering crop extremely profitable, it also led to the growth of slavery. In 1790, the slave population in the United States was 697,897. By 1810, almost 20 years after Whitney's invention, the slave population had grown to 1.2 million. As cotton production soared, it became more unlikely that African Americans would gain their freedom, something many had hoped for after the American Revolution. While some people viewed the cotton gin as progress, it represented something far more tragic, too.

Inventing the Cotton Gin

Whitney knew there was no time to waste. In Great Britain, new inventions such as sewing and weaving machines were ready to make American cotton into fabric. He quickly observed that a machine that separated the sticky seeds from the fluffy fiber could help. Machines worked faster than people, which would in turn raise profits.

Whitney went to work with his partner, Phineas Miller, in 1793. In just 10 days, Whitney had designed a basic machine he called the cotton gin. "Gin" was short for the word "engine." His machine separated seeds from fibers 10 times faster than a person doing the work by hand. A small model of his gin was cranked by hand. Larger models could be powered by a horse or the movement of water.

The Parts

The first **version** of Whitney's cotton gin had four basic parts. A part called a hopper was where a person loaded the cotton into the machine. From there, a spinning tube covered with hundreds of wire hooks moved the cotton through and along the third part, which was a **stationary** surface. This separated the seeds from the fluffy cotton fiber. Finally, the clearer, a tube covered with bristles, spun in the opposite direction to brush the cotton off the hooks.

hand crank

bristles

hopper

hooks

Whitney showed the first model of his cotton gin to a group of friends. He was able to complete an entire day's work cleaning cotton in just one hour.

Patents and Problems

As he built his cotton gin, Whitney had his future in mind. He knew that he could send his design to the U.S. government and get a special license called a **patent**. At the time, patents ensured that the patent holder had the only rights to their invention for 14 years. Whitney hoped he could make money from his invention.

Whitney received a patent for his machine in 1794. He and Phineas Miller didn't sell their cotton gins, but offered to process cotton for farmers for a share of their profits. This made farmers angry, and soon, people began copying Whitney's design without his permission. When he saw that he was losing money, Whitney tried to take the issue to court, but he didn't have much luck.

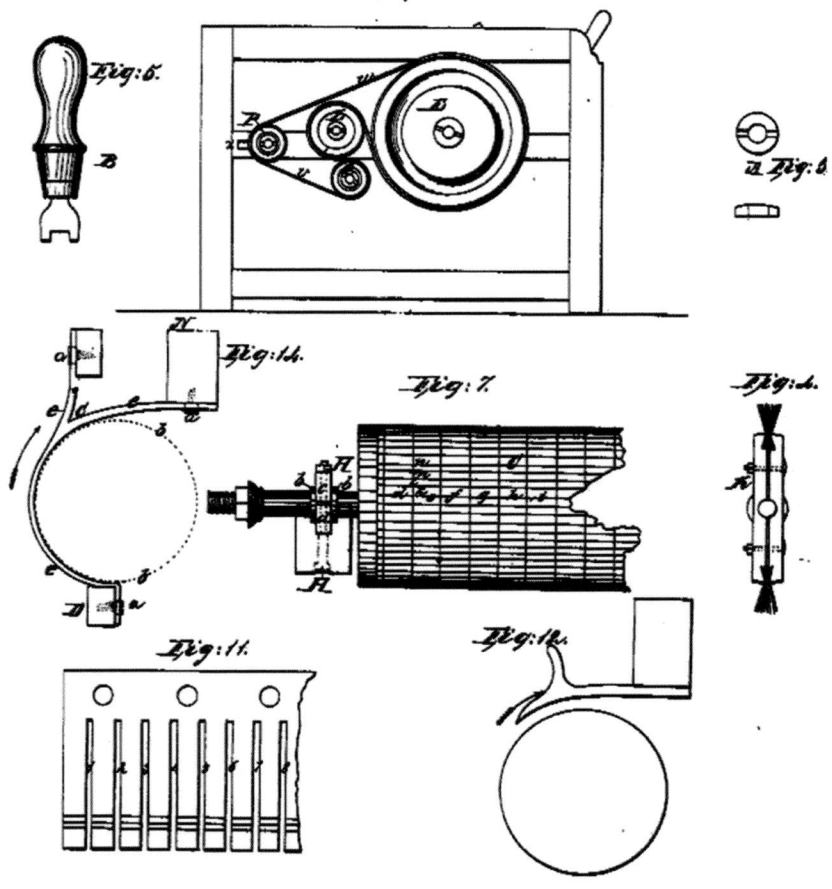

72X

E. Whitney,
Cotton Gin.
Patented Mar. 14, 1794.

2 Sheets - Sheet 2.

Fig: 8.

Fig: 5.

Fig: 6.

Fig: 14.

Fig: 7.

Fig: 10.

Fig: 11.

Fig: 12.

Believe it or not, Whitney's cotton gin didn't make him rich.
By 1797, Whitney and Miller were out of business.

A New Start and New Ideas

Disappointed in the outcome of the cotton gin business, Whitney moved back to New England. Though his business had failed, he was not ready to give up. In 1798, he learned the U.S. government needed private contractors to manufacture muskets for the army. At this time, guns were made by hand, one at a time. Each weapon was unique, and parts couldn't be shared between guns.

Whitney believed machines could be used to produce guns more quickly. He was also determined to find a way to make **interchangeable parts**. Confident in his idea, Whitney pledged to make 10,000 guns for the army in two years. Coming from anyone else, this idea would've seemed crazy. But the government had faith in Whitney, who was known for his **innovative** cotton gin.

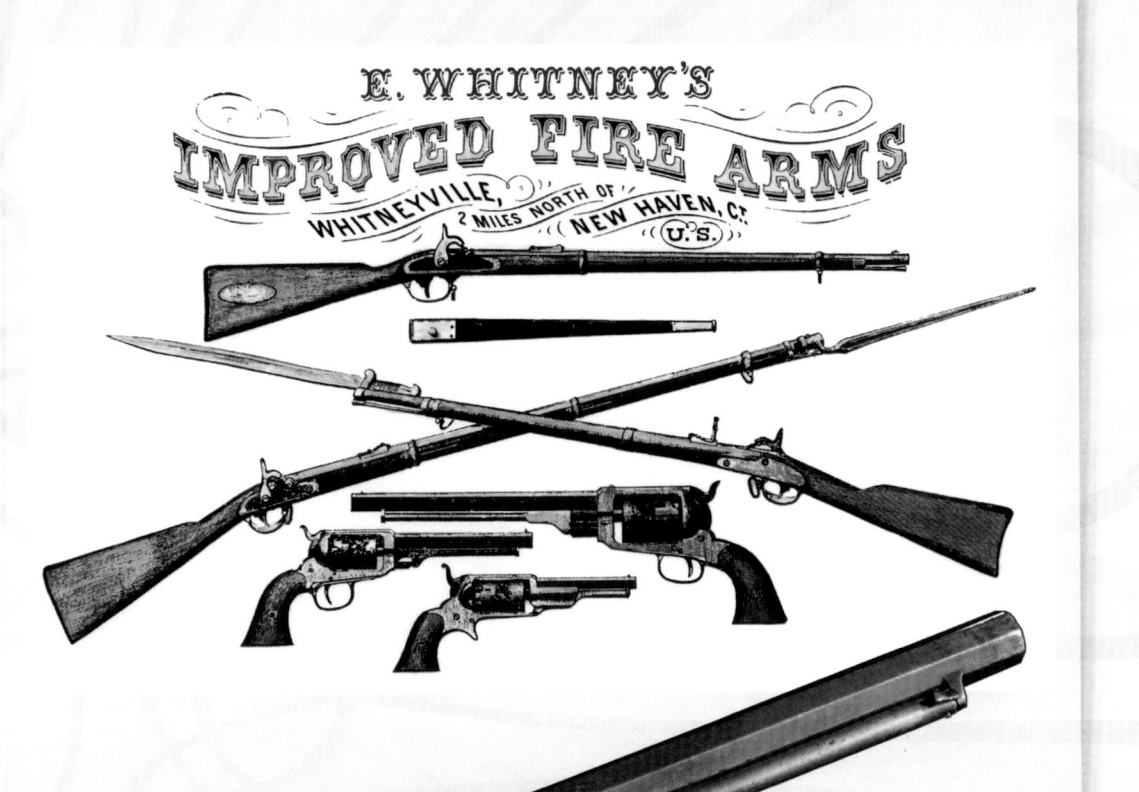

Although Whitney promised to deliver 10,000 guns in two years, it actually took him about 10 years to make good on his contract.

Manufacturing Muskets

First, Whitney came up with a design for a musket. Then, he made a template, or model, for each of its parts. Using these templates, anybody could make the parts and assemble a musket. This revolutionary idea changed manufacturing forever—now, even unskilled laborers could make items that were once limited to highly trained craftsmen.

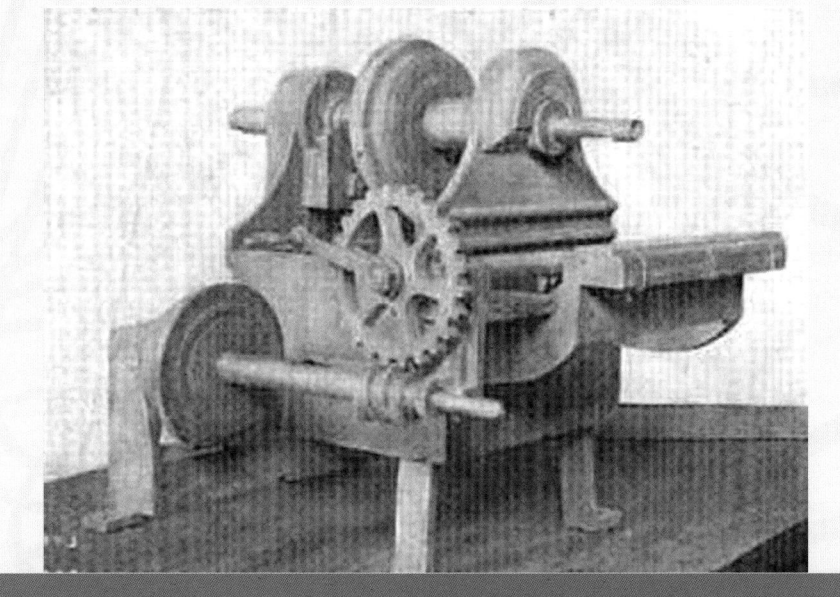

Some people credit Whitney with producing the first true milling machine, though the process it used existed before his invention. This milling machine is an early version of the technology.

Whitney didn't just stop at designing a musket. He also invented a machine that people could use to make its parts. It was called a milling machine. It allowed the operator to cut metal according to a template. All they had to do was clamp the metal to a table and lay the template on top of it. The milling machine followed the outline of the template. It didn't require great skill like traditional metalworking did.

Shaping Industries

As an entrepreneur, Whitney stands out because he didn't always have original ideas. He didn't invent the idea of interchangeable parts—it had existed long before him. He wasn't an experienced gun maker, and he didn't invent the milling technique. However, he developed these ideas and was able to make them succeed on a large scale.

Whitney's ideas had a great influence on manufacturing in the United States. Previously, it took a lot of time and skill to create many goods. Now, unskilled laborers could create these goods more quickly and less expensively. This would pave the way for mass production, or producing large amounts of goods with machines. It's a system still used in factories today.

Inventors, engineers, and entrepreneurs are constantly finding ways to make already existing ideas better, faster, or cheaper.

23

Forming a Factory

When Whitney signed a contract to make muskets for the U.S. government, he took a big chance. He agreed to make a lot of weapons, but he didn't have any experience making them. He didn't even have workers or a factory! However, he immediately set to work building a factory at Mill Rock, which is near New Haven, Connecticut. The main part of Whitney's factory was built by 1799.

Like he did with previous inventions, Whitney took techniques he had heard about and adapted them for his factory. He built his own tools and developed machines that could be powered by water, which he said would "greatly **diminish** the labor" needed to build his goods.

Part of Whitney's business plan was to build a factory where he made the machines that would be used to manufacture muskets. This 1827 painting shows the Eli Whitney Gun Factory, which was also known as the Whitney **Armory**, located along the Mill River.

Learning Lessons

Whitney was successful in part because he didn't easily give up on ideas. One time, he saw that Catherine Greene used a needlework frame that tore her threads. Although Whitney was not familiar with needlework, he gave the problem some thought. Before long, he invented a frame that solved Greene's problem. Though not a farmer himself, he identified what cotton farmers needed and built a solution. When faced with the idea of making muskets, he studied them until he knew enough to efficiently make thousands of them.

Eli Whitney's entrepreneurial spirit greatly influenced American manufacturing and the American economy. Just as the cotton gin transformed the economy in the South, his manufacturing methods transformed the North's factory-based economy. His influence has lasted well after his death in 1825.

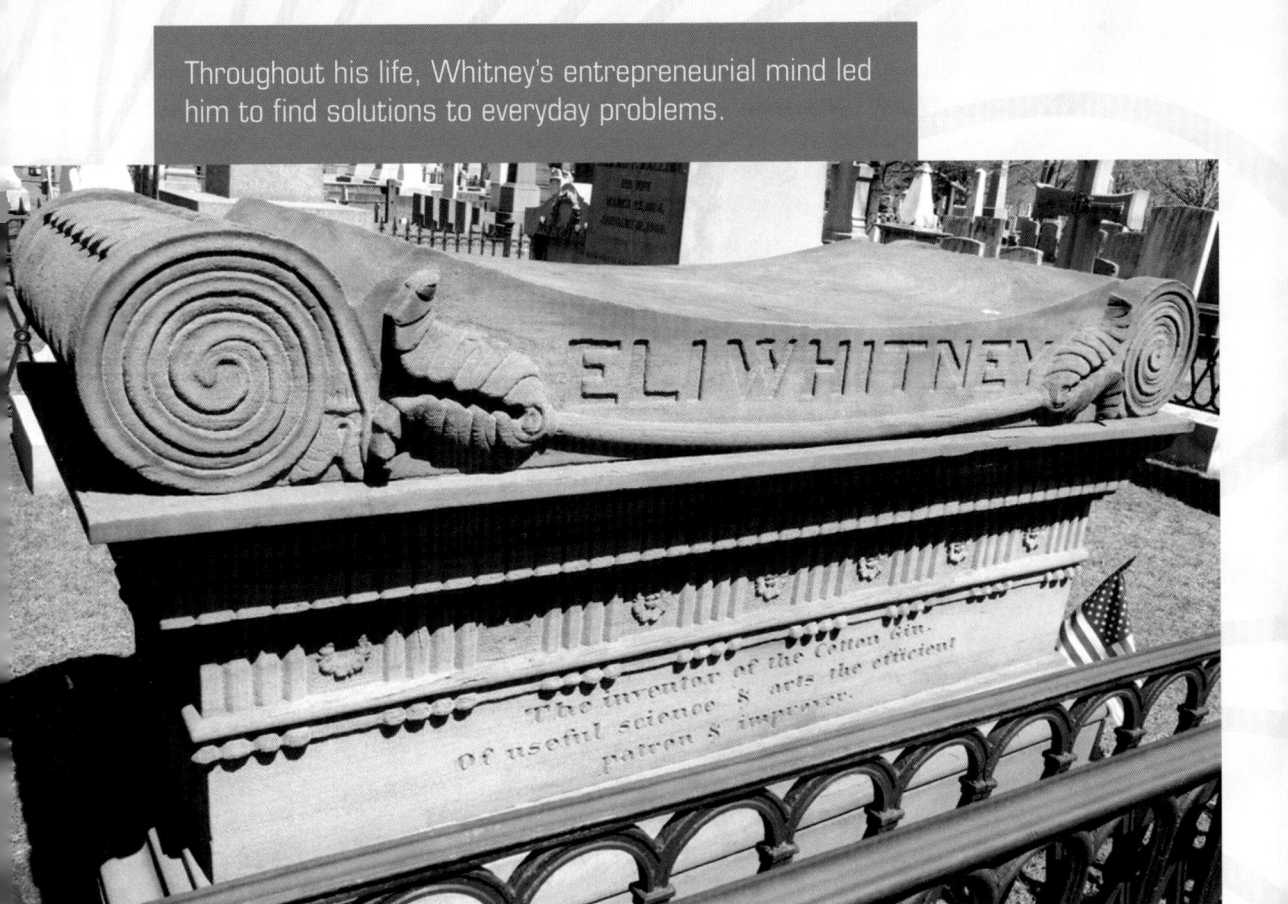

Throughout his life, Whitney's entrepreneurial mind led him to find solutions to everyday problems.

ELI WHITNEY

The inventor of the Cotton Gin. Of useful science & arts the efficient patron & improver.

Family Life

Eli Whitney did not get married until he was 52. In 1817, he met and married Henrietta Edwards. They had four children. His only son, Eli Whitney Jr., was born in 1820. Unfortunately, Whitney died when his son was only four years old. The younger Whitney took over his father's manufacturing business in 1842 and carried out his legacy of entrepreneurship. Like his father, he had a mind for business, and the Whitney Armory remained profitable for decades.

Changing Lives

Over the course of his life, Whitney learned from his experiences, educating himself and learning from his mistakes. Eventually, his hard work and determination paid off and allowed him to live comfortably. Today, his name is familiar because his inventions and ideas changed lives.

Whitney's inventions made it possible for people without much experience or many technical abilities to find work and make a living. Whitney's ideas allowed the northern states to become a center of manufacturing with a reputation that was known around the world. And his inventions changed the economy of a nation when southern farmers were at last able to able profit from cotton. Thanks to Eli Whitney's entrepreneurship, the United States was changed forever.

The rise of American manufacturing is due in part to Eli Whitney's creative thinking.

29

A Timeline of Eli Whitney's Life

1765 — Eli Whitney is born near Westboro, Massachusetts.

1775-1783 — The American Revolution is fought in the American colonies. Whitney runs a profitable nail business from his father's shop.

1775-1783 — Whitney attends Yale College in Connecticut.

1792 — Whitney moves to Georgia, where he meets Catherine Greene and Phineas Miller.

1793 — Whitney invents the cotton gin.

1794 — Whitney receives a patent for the cotton gin.

1797 — Whitney and Miller go out of business.

1798 — Whitney signs a contract with the U.S. government to produce 10,000 muskets in two years. Whitney develops a milling machine.

1799 — Whitney completes construction on his factory near New Haven, Connecticut.

1817 — Whitney marries Henrietta Edwards.

1820 — Eli Whitney Jr. is born.

1825 — Whitney dies in New Haven, Connecticut.

1842 — Eli Whitney Jr. takes over the Whitney Armory.

Glossary

armory: A place where arms, or weapons and ammunition, are manufactured or stored.

boll: A rounded case that contains seeds in plants such as cotton and flax.

diminish: To reduce.

industry: Economic activity concerned with processing raw materials or creating goods.

innovative: Advanced and original.

interchangeable parts: Parts that are made to be identical so that they can replace each other in any kind of assembly.

knack: Natural talent.

musket: A kind of gun with a long barrel.

patent: Rights given to a person by the government to make, use, or sell an invention.

profit: Financial gain.

stationary: Fixed in one place.

textile: A type of cloth or woven fabric.

version: One form of something.

Index

Websites

Due to the changing nature of Internet links, PowerKids Press has developed an online list of websites related to the subject of this book. This site is updated regularly. Please use this link to access the list: www.powerkidslinks.com/entre/eliw